Casa Masó

Noucentista Life and Architecture

1912

Casa Masó

Noucentista Life and Architecture

Edited by
Jordi Falgàs

Texts by
Narcís-Jordi Aragó Masó
Jordi Falgàs
Rosa M. Gil Tort

Photographs by
Jordi Puig

TRIANGLE ▼ POSTALS

© **Published by**
Fundació Rafael Masó
Triangle Postals

First edition, April 2012, Girona and Sant Lluís.

Edited by Jordi Falgàs

Text
Narcís-Jordi Aragó Masó
Jordi Falgàs
Rosa M. Gil Tort

© **Photography**
Jordi Puig,
except when another author, origin or owner is indicated.

Design
Joan Barjau

Layout
Vador Minobis

Translation from catalan
Steve Cedar

All the works reproduced are by Rafael Masó Valentí,
except when otherwise indicated.

Printed by
Tallers Gràfics Hostench SA

Printed in Barcelona

Legal reg. no.: GI-280-2012
ISBN: 978-84-8496-170-3

Fundació Rafael Masó
Girona
Tel. +34 972 413 989
info@rafaelmaso.org

Triangle Postals SL
Sant Lluís, Menorca
Tel. +34 971 150 451
triangle@triangle.cat

www.triangle.cat
www.rafaelmaso.org

Contents

Passer-by who brushes past these shaded, bare, deep brown walls of our house, sink your keen and curious eye a little further inside of this exterior; perhaps here you will find everything your soul longs for and your eyes are aware of.

—

Rafael Masó, 1917

The cession of the Masó House to the city of Girona (2006) and the remodelling of the building (2007-2011) have been two basic steps to set into motion the Fundació Rafael Masó. The first step means that now this house belongs to all the citizens of Girona, and the second step shows that the City Council has wanted all the people of Girona, and all those who visit it, to be able to discover and have available to them this so important piece of historical and artistic heritage. Its conservation, study and popularising would not make any sense if it were not at the disposition of the public. Thus with the completion of the remodelling works and turning of the Masó House into a museum, the time has come for the people of Girona to begin to enjoy a new cultural facility that is theirs and which, as such, must respond to their needs and interests.

The architecture of Rafael Masó constitutes a fundamental chapter in the construction of a modern and European Girona and, one hundred years later, the legacy of *Noucentisme* urges us to continue working for a more cultured and freer country. For this we must thank, once again, the generosity of Narcís-Jordi Aragó Masó and Mercè Huerta Busquets when ceding this legacy to their city, which they love so much, and we must reaffirm our commitment to preserve it for future generations.

Carles Puigdemont i Casamajó
Mayor of Girona and President of the Fundació Rafael Masó

The architecture of Rafael Masó in *noucentista* Catalonia

Jordi Falgàs

But you hide, Girona,
in your womb the young
enamored Architect.

—

Eugeni d'Ors, 1911[1]

Noucentisme is largely unknown, both inside and outside of Catalonia.[2] It was a movement considered anti-modern because it championed classicism and tradition and, therefore, was exiled from the history of modernity. However, the revision of monolithic views of the historiographical canon has enabled us to reclaim movements such as *Noucentisme*, which developed in the asynchronous, decentralized and hybrid periphery of the modern world.[3]

Just like other emerging cultural phenomena in the early 20th century, *Noucentisme* arose from the catholic, nationalist and conservative ideological substrata of a social class that for the first time had the economic power to achieve a certain amount of political independence in post-colonial Spain.[4] *Noucentisme* was a movement that dominated a large part of the arts, thought and politics in Catalonia during the second decade of the 20th century, and while it promoted the modernization and Europeanization of the country it also championed a mythologized vision of the Greco-Latin substrata of Catalan culture and, generally, of the history of Catalonia.[5] It was a movement of the middle classes, above all of the new urban bourgeoisie, which had to face the pressure of the organized

Fig. 1

Masó-Puig Pharmacy, Girona, shelves and benches of the interior.

working class at the same time as it achieved political and economic power in Catalonia.

The emergence and development of *Noucentisme* was also closely linked to *Modernisme*, the movement that had blossomed in Catalan arts and humanities at the end of the 19th century being influenced by Impressionism and French Art Nouveau. The austerity, order and civility that *Noucentisme* proposed was to a large extent a reaction to everything that was perceived as the excesses of *Modernisme*, but the fact is that both movements also had coinciding points and coexisted for some years. In reality, many artists and writers evolved from *Modernisme* towards *Noucentisme* without making big breaks or regrets. It is in this context that Rafael Masó i Valentí (1880-1935) was born and educated, in a conservative, catholic, pro-Catalan autonomy and enlightened family from Girona.[6]

The cultured atmosphere provided by the literary and artistic interests of his father, as well as the love of the city and its traditions, marked both the personality and path of the future architect. An admirer of Antoni Gaudí, during his studies in Barcelona Masó joined the group of artists and writers who wanted to create an alternative to the ruling styles, whether they were the official eclecticisms or historicisms or the exuberance of *Modernisme*. The civic attitude, Catalan nationalism and the modernizing and pro-European nature that *Noucentisme* promoted meant that Masó also distinguished himself as a poet, urban planner, politician and promoter of art and literature.

Masó always worked in Girona. That is why the majority of his buildings are in the city and its area of influence. As well as houses, chalets and apartment blocks, he designed

Fig. 2

Reform project of an apartment building for Lluís Batlle, Fontanilles street facade elevation, Girona, 1909. Pencil and watercolor on paper, 29.5 x 23 cm. Historical Archive of the Col·legi d'Arquitectes de Catalunya – Demarcació de Girona, reg. no. 9510-13.

all kinds of buildings, from schools and hospitals to factories and shops.[7] He also worked on reforming country houses and on the restoration of medieval architecture. From his period as an architecture student, Masó always showed an interest in certain tendencies of recent European architecture, above all the British Arts & Crafts movement and the new central European regionalist architecture, and his architecture fits in with regionalist currents where the architects sought out the elements to create a national architecture from the local and regional traditions.[8] In his restorations and new buildings, in the interiors and in the ornamental objects that he designed, Masó adopted a series of materials and techniques taken from vernacular architecture (especially glazed and black ceramics, wrought iron, stone, wood and stucco) but used them in an innovative way without precedents in Catalonia, thanks above all to the introduction of formal and functional elements that he found simultaneously in early Greco-Roman architecture and in modern British and German architecture.

Masó completed his architecture studies in 1906, when the philosopher Eugeni d'Ors had begun publishing the "Glossari," a daily opinion column in *La Veu de Catalunya* from which he christened, defined and led *Noucentisme*. At the same time, Enric Prat de la Riba published *La nacionalitat catalana*, a book of nationalist doctrine that together with the aesthetic theses of Ors brought together the first generation of *noucentista* intellectuals and artists.

Fig. 3

Mas El Soler, Sant Hilari Sacalm, entrance hall, 1910.

Fig. 4

Teixidor Flour Mill, Girona, iron fence and entrance gate to the house, 1910-11. Photo by Adolf Mas, 1916, courtesy Fundació Institut Amatller d'Art Hispànic, Arxiu Mas, Barcelona.

As an expression of a generation who worked simultaneously in different fields of art and politics, and from different places around Catalonia, architecture was an ideal vehicle to express the *noucentista* ideals, since it was connected to the growth of the cities, to the creation of infrastructures and public facilities (libraries, schools, parks, cemeteries), to artistic and craft production (mural painting and public sculpture), and to the desire for social cohesion in order to consolidate bourgeois hegemony.

Pushed by what had happened in Barcelona, at the turn of the century Girona had also begun its enlargement, knocking down city walls and opening up streets that had to enable the construction of buildings organized by a new group of businessmen and landowners. From these early years of Masó's professional life, what stands out are works marked by Gaudinism and *modernista* organicism, such as the Masó-Puig Pharmacy in Girona (1908, fig. 1). In the reform project of an apartment building for Lluís Batlle, in Girona (1909), there already appear the first signs of an austere monumentality and ornamentation (fig. 2).

The reform works on the El Soler country house (1909, fig. 3) gave him the chance to intervene globally in a large farmhouse, in dialogue with vernacular architecture and introducing new elements of organization of space and interior decoration to it. The geometric stylization of the forms, the chromatic sobriety of the materials, the stripping

Fig. 5

Athenea, Girona, facade, 1913. Photo by Adolf Mas, 1916, courtesy Fundació Institut Amatller d'Art Hispànic, Arxiu Mas, Barcelona.

of the spaces and the preponderance of traditional craft techniques that Masó had discovered studying the work of architects such as Charles F. A. Voysey, Mackay Hugh Baillie Scott and Charles Rennie Mackintosh gradually took on prominence in works such as the Teixidor Flour Factory in Girona (1910, fig. 4), the altar of the church of Sant Salvador de Bianya (1911), the Ensesa warehouse in Girona (1911), and the reform of the Masó house (1911); as well as in the furniture he designed for the Coll house in Borrassà (1909) and for his own home (1910-1912).

In 1911 Ors stressed his leadership promoting the publication of the *Almanach dels Noucentistes* (in which Masó was present as a poet), and counting on the well-informed opinions about art and decoration of Joaquim Folch i Torres as writer of the "*Pàgina Artística*" of *La Veu de Catalunya*. Painters such as Joaquim Torres García and Joaquim Sunyer, sculptors such as Enric Casanovas, and poets such as Josep Carner and Josep M. López-Picó also reached critical moments in their creative work in perfect tuning with the *noucentista* postulates. The political leadership of Prat de la Riba, first as President of the Province of Barcelona and from 1914 of the *Mancomunitat* (Catalonia's semi-autonomous government), made it possible to start a program of creation and modernization of public, cultural and educational infrastructures where *noucentista* architecture was particularly relevant, from the hand of other architects such as Josep Puig i Cadafalch, Lluís Planas Calvet, Josep M. Pericas, Josep Goday, Ignasi Mas, Eduard M. Balcells, Francesc Folguera, Ramon Puig Gairalt and Josep Danés, among others.

In Masó's case the journey he made in 1912 for his honeymoon with Esperança Bru was decisive. On the route he took, among other places, to the Darmstadt Artists'

Colony and the Garden City of Hellerau, on the outskirts of Dresden, Masó was able to experience close-up the buildings and furnishings of the most outstanding figures of German and Austrian architecture: Joseph Maria Olbrich, Richard Riemerschmid, Hermann Muthesius, Heinrich Tessenow, and Peter Behrens. Their formal innovations, as well as the importance of the dialogue between the buildings and their natural and cultural settings, and the collaboration between architects, sculptors and craftsmen convinced Masó that he was on the right tracks.

In 1912 Masó began a period of five years in which his most significant works are concentrated. In Girona he led the Athenea cultural association, for which he designed an exhibition and concert hall which, in the words of Tarrús and Comadira, can be interpreted as a "manifesto of *noucentista* architecture" (fig. 5).[9] The period in which Athenea operated, from 1913 to 1917, coincides with the greatest *noucentista* effervescence in Girona due to a large extent to the relationship Masó had with the leading literary and artistic figures of the movement.[10] This period features his projects for the reform of the Cendra House in Anglès (1913) and the Ensesa House in Girona (1913); and his most prominent new buildings, the Masramon House in Olot (1913, fig. 6) and the Casas House, on the outskirts of Sant Feliu de Guíxols (1914).

In 1917 *Noucentisme* suffered its first crisis closely linked to the ideological, economic, political and social fracture that all Spain experienced, and to the effects of World War I. The death of Prat de la Riba and the successive distancing from Catalonia of figures such as Ors, Carner and Torres García demonstrate a stagnation of the movement, which languished during the dictatorship of General Primo de

Fig. 6

Masramon House, Olot, main facade (east), 1913-15. Photo by Adolf Mas, 1916, courtesy Fundació Institut Amatller d'Art Hispànic, Arxiu Mas, Barcelona.

Rivera, between 1923 and 1930. Masó's architectural work also noted the crisis of *Noucentisme*, although he continued receiving many commissions for all types of buildings and reforms. One of his most ambitious projects, which he could not see completed, was the garden city of S'Agaró, a summer resort in the heart of the Costa Brava on which he worked from 1923, based on an original idea from 1917 (fig. 7).

Masó wanted to unite the tradition of vernacular architecture with new ideas about the structure and ornamentation of buildings, interior decoration, and furniture design. Unfortunately, he often came up against incomprehension or rejection of his proposals, and his projects did not go past the paper stage or were unfinished. Moreover, after his death some buildings were knocked down or irreparably altered, something that has made the study and interpretation of his work more difficult. However, his contribution was decisive for the introduction into Catalonia of modern concepts in architectural design, urban planning and growth (the holiday chalet, the garden city), the renovation of craftsmanship (new methods of production and use), the conservation of the historical heritage, and the need to democratize the study of and access to the arts (with the creation of Athenea and an Arts and Crafts School in Girona).[11]

Fig. 7.

La Gavina Hostel, S'Agaró, with the Domus Nostrum chalet in the background, 1932. Photo by Adolf Zerkowitz, c. 1932. Historic Archive of the Col·legi d'Arquitectes de Catalunya – Demarcació de Girona, reg. 7539 c.3 c.155.

Masó's work is distinguished by the full identification with the *noucentista* postulates of a modernity that defended the most austere classicism and yet it integrated forms, colors and materials of the culture itself, reclaiming the nobility and moral value of craftsmanship. For this reason we can state that, in his attempt to develop a modern vernacular architecture, Masó embodies the attempt of *Noucentisme* to reconcile the adoption of international modernism with the preservation of local identity and traditions.

1 "Però tu amagues, Girona, en ton si el jove Arquitecte amorós." Eugeni d'Ors [Xènius, pseud.], "Elogi de Girona," 3 November, 1911, in Ors, *Glosari 1910-1911*, ed. Xavier Pla (Barcelona: Quaderns Crema, 2003), 774.

2 The term *Noucentisme* literally means the ism of the 900s, that is, of the 20th century. This article includes fragments of my doctoral dissertation. See Jordi Falgàs, "Modernity and Tradition in Catalan Noucentisme: Rafael Masó's Regionalist Architecture, 1911-1917" (PhD diss., University of Wisconsin-Madison, 2011).

3 See Marshall Berman, *All That Is Solid Melts into Air: The Experience of Modernity* (New York: Penguin, 1988, 2a. ed.).

4 See Carl E. Schorske, *Fin-de-Siècle Vienna: Politics and Culture* (New York: Knopf, 1980), and Debora L. Silverman, *Art Nouveau in Fin-de-Siècle France* (Berkeley: California, 1989). The works of Kenneth Silver and Romy Golan are also essential for the study of specific cultural phenomena in art in the early 20th century.

5 See Martí Peran, Alícia Suàrez, and Mercè Vidal, eds. *El Noucentisme: un projecte de modernitat* (Barcelona: Generalitat de Catalunya / Enciclopèdia Catalana / Centre de Cultura Contemporània de Barcelona, 1994); and Oriol Bohigas *et al.*, *El Noucentisme*, Història de la cultura catalana, vol. 7 (Barcelona: Edicions 62, 1996).

6 See Joan Tarrús and Narcís Comadira, *Rafael Masó: arquitecte noucentista* (Girona: Brau / Col·legi d'Arquitectes de Catalunya, 2007, 2nd ed.). The monograph by Tarrús and Comadira is the most complete study about the life and work of Masó.

7 See the catalogue by Raquel Lacuesta *et al.*, *Rafael Masó i Valentí: Arquitecte (1880-1935)* (Barcelona: Fundació "la Caixa", 2006).

8 See Anthony Alofsin, *When Buildings Speak: Architecture as Language in the Habsburg Empire and Its Aftermath, 1867-1933* (Chicago: University of Chicago Press, 2006).

9 Tarrús and Comadira, 172.

10 See Narcís-Jordi Aragó, *Rafael Masó i els noucentistes: Epistolari* (Girona: Diputació de Girona, 2007).

11 See Falgàs, "A Catalan Werkstätte? Arts and Crafts Schools between *Modernisme* and *Noucentisme*," *Journal of Modern Craft* 2 (November 2009): 285-93.

History of the Masó family in their home

Rosa M. Gil Tort

The origin of Ballesteries Street in Girona is in the sandy ground at the foot of the Roman wall in la Força Street, the ancient Via Augusta. The first houses of this sector were built in the 13th century. They had courtyards and orchards in front, and the street was closed by two portals, one at the level of the current Pujada de Sant Feliu and the other in Quatre Cantons. In the 14th century the street took on the name of arrow and crossbow craftsmen, for whom the closeness to the river made their work easier. During the siege of 1462, all the houses in the street were knocked down to defend la Força Vella, and the current buildings date mainly from the early 16th century (fig. 1).[1] In fact the spaces of the houses knocked down for the siege were used to redirect the royal way towards Ballesteries, which until then had passed through la Força Street. The road meant the opening of workshops of carriages, carters and horseshoe makers, and conditioned a gradual and homogeneous urbanism.

The houses with odd numbers, beside the river, corresponded —and some still belong to them today— to craftsmen with a shop and workshop on the ground floor; and the higher floors have always been used as popular housing. We find the exception to the rule in the Masó House, an example of bourgeois housing from at least the mid-19th century. The even-numbered houses are also

Fig. 1

Ballesteries Street, today.

an evolution of the old medieval trades, but on the upper floors many of the houses are, in reality, the facade of the back of the medieval manor houses of la Força Street.

Lives under the same roof

The Masó House was linked to the same family for almost 180 years, from the mid-19th century until the early 21st century. The sociological profile of its dwellers —liberal professionals of medicine, law, pharmacy, architecture and journalism— has meant the conservation of a large part of their furniture. Beyond its worth as heritage, the house is a fine example of the emergence of a bourgeois middle class from rural capitals where the passing on of property interwove the intellectual capital with the agricultural income and some economic contributions resulting from overseas trade. The house has undergone many changes, from a watchmaker's workshop and barber-surgeon's shop in the 19th century to becoming the headquarters of the Fundació Rafael Masó, as well as being the home where the architect Rafael Masó was born.

The first of the four properties that were transformed into the current Masó House was Ballesteries number 31, and was bought by Francesc de Paula Montaña Blasi (1802-1874) on the 21 August 1845. It was the rented home of Paula Cargol Menta, widow of Pere Fuster, surgeon, and married a second time to Francesc de Paula Montaña. Montaña was from the village of Llers and studied in Barcelona, principally humanities and philosophy. In 1826 he graduated in surgery, and in 1828 in medicine, and came to Girona in 1828 or 1829.[2] In 1840 he was named surgical doctor of the National Militia, and he practiced as a doctor and surgeon simultaneously in the Hospital of Santa Caterina and the charity institutions in general. According to the inventory of the furniture existing when the marriage contract was draw up between Francesc Montaña and Paula Cargol, in 1833, and from the description of the objects found in the shop of the house, everything indicates that it was a barber-surgery establishment, professions that in the early 19th century differed little.[3] The furniture was inherited by Narcisa Fuster Cargol, the owner's stepdaughter.[4]

The next family who lived in the house was that of Jaume Valentí Rovira (1826-1874), a doctor from Vilanova i la Geltrú who married Narcisa Fuster in 1850. In 1854 Jaume Valentí was named physician of the artillery company of Girona and also worked as a civilian doctor. The couple had two daughters: Gertrudis and Paula, who some years later would be the mother of the architect Rafael Masó.

The Masó family was originally from Sitges, where in 1784 Rafael Masó Font and Rosalia Pascual had been married. Their son Rafael Masó Pascual emigrated to Cuba, and there he married Teresa Ruiz de Espejo Castellanos, from Santiago de Cuba. The couple had four children: Rafael, Rosalia, Gaudenci and Frederic. The father of the family worked in maritime trade as a broker for the ships on the route between Barcelona and Santiago de Cuba.[5] Around 1840 they moved to Barcelona, and in 1852 Rafael Masó founded Rafael Masó and Co., which continued operating on the Barcelona-Santiago de Cuba route, since he had kept some sailboats of the Cuban company, such as the *Rosalía* and the *Paquete de Sitges*.

Gaudenci Masó Ruiz de Espejo (1830-1893), as well as the merchant businesses, was councillor and deputy mayor of Barcelona City Council for the Liberal Party (fig. 2). In 1850

he married Paula Pagès Monserdà, and the marriage produced six children: Rafael, Maturo, Rosalia, Alfons, and the twins Francesc de Paula and Carme. Gaudenci Masó also had an artistic leaning and went to painting classes in the Llotja art school, in the period when the Nazarene painter Claudi Lorenzale taught.[6] On the death of his wife Paula in 1866, aged 35, he moved to Girona, where she had property, since she was the only daughter of Narcís Pagès Oliver Rosselló, a lawyer in Barcelona and from a family of Girona landowners. Gaudenci Masó married for the second time Rosa Sagristà Amat, with whom he did not have children. They lived in l'Escola Pia Street. In 1881 Gaudenci founded the newspaper *El Constitucional: periódico liberal*, which was first published in 1889; and in 1890, a few years before he died, he had been appointed official of the Second Chamber of the Courts of Girona.[7]

Rafael (1851-1915), the first-born of Gaudenci Masó and Paula Pagès, was born in Barcelona but did his secondary education in Girona and then went to Bologna to study law. In Italy he became interested in painting, and throughout his life he was an amateur painter and a modest collector. When he returned from Bologna, without having completed his studies, he worked as a solicitor and administrator. In 1877 he married Paula Valentí (1851-1926) and they went to live in the house in Ballesteries, which she had inherited from her mother. The couple had eleven children: Santiago (1878-1960), Rafael, the architect; Artur (1882-1882), Joan (1883-1973), Francesc de Paula (1885-1902), Àngela (1886-1960), Josep (1887-1887), Alfons (1889-1889), Narcís (1890-1953), Maria de la Bonanova (1892-1981) and Paula (1894-1957) (fig. 3). As the family increased in size, during the latter decades of the century, Rafael Masó Pagès bought the houses alongside his own,

Fig. 2

Portrait of Gaudenci Masó, undated. Photographer unknown. Fundació Rafael Masó Archive, reg. image no. 10.

Fig. 3

The Masó Valentí family, c. 1896. From left to right, standing, Francesc, Rafael, Angelina, the father, Santiago, Maria, Joan and Narcís. Seated, the mother, with Paula on her lap. Photographer unknown. Fundació Rafael Masó Archive, reg. image no. 64.

so that he ended up being the owner of numbers 31, 33 and 35, which are the properties that his architect son joined and remodelled in 1911.

On the 28 September 1889 Rafael Masó Pagès published the first issue of *Diario de Gerona de avisos y noticias*, two weeks after the last issue of his father's *El Constitucional* appeared, and he directed it until his death in 1915 (fig. 4). Unlike his predecessor, Rafael Masó Pagès bought printing machinery and set up a press on the ground floor of the Masó House, to print both the newspaper and to provide general printing services of books and all types of documents.[8] Despite the work on the newspaper, the printing press and his love of painting, Rafael Masó Pagès never abandoned his profession as solicitor and was dean of the Solicitors Professional Association, councillor on Girona

REDACCIÓN ADMINISTRACIÓN E IMPRENTA

DIARIO DE GERONA DE AVISOS Y NOTICIAS

SUSCRIPCIÓN

Año XXVIII Núm. 80 Miércoles 5 de abril de 1916

Bicarbonato de sosa químicamente puro

DE TORRES MUÑOZ-S. Marcos 11.-Madrid

De venta en Gerona; Farmacia Almeda, Platería 29.

AGUA DE SOLARES

PROVEEDOR DE LA REAL CASA

Depósito y de venta en Gerona

Farmacia Almeda, Platería 29

NOTAS DE LA GUERRA

Opinión francesa

La Conferencia reunida en París parece haber unido en un solo pensamiento a los aliados, hacia la unidad de miras y de propósitos que ha tiempo persiguen, con el acicate de la que reina entre sus adversarios.

Sin embargo, al lado de esa actitud, que podemos llamar oficial, bueno es consultar la que también podemos llamar opinión popular, pulsando sus latidos en las columnas de la prensa francesa, al través de los rigores de la censura con que lucha, de la que hallamos un eco digno de ser recogido en *Le Journal*, en un artículo que subscribe Carlos Humbert, con motivo de la reciente movilización de parte del reemplazo de 1888.

Por el momento quedan exceptuados del llamamiento los padres de familia, y se asegura que los llamados se destinarán en primer lugar, a reemplazar a los obreros de administración militar que sirven todavía a retaguardia y serán enviados al frente, y, en segundo lugar, a servir en las fábricas y talleres del interior.

«Tales precauciones —escribe el articulista— no pueden atenuar la crudeza del hecho. Cualquiera que sea su destino, esos hombres se ven apartados de sus hogares y de sus negocios. Además se vislumbran nuevos llamamientos y se habla ya de que los obreros especialistas de los reemplazos de 1916 y 1917, hasta el presente en los talleres, deberán abandonarlos en 1.° de junio próximo. De este modo, pese a la aparente moderación de las medidas tomadas y de los circunloquios empleados, es lo cierto que nuestras reservas de hombres van empobreciéndose...»

Las mismas razones que motivan la movilización de la primera parte del reclutamiento de 1888 y el llamamiento de los obreros de 1916 y 1917, servirán, en sentir del colega transpirenaico, para llamar a la segunda parte y a los obreros de 1915 y 1914 y así sucesivamente.

«Con este sistema —dice— todos los franceses, cualquiera que sea su edad, serán alcanzados por la movilización.»

Este estado de cosas inspira al escritor francés los siguientes comentarios:

«Indudablemente, si la salud nacional exigiese, imperiosamente, este supremo esfuerzo, nadie en nuestro país tendría nada que decir, y yo sería el primero en decirlo. Pero, ya que nos hallamos rodeados de aliados prontos á poner sus sacrificios a la altura de los nuestros, ¿por qué hemos de seguir haciendo frente, casi solos, a las obligaciones, cuya carga más pesada hemos sobrellevado hasta ahora?

Ha sido Francia, a pesar de la insuficiencia de su preparación, la primera en oponer a la empresa alemana una fuerza constituída capaz de mantener en jaque la potencia germánica; la que ha hecho abortar con su magnífica resistencia el plan alemán; la que, después de veinte meses, tiene á raya las mejores y más numerosas tropas del adversario, cuyas reservas de reclutamiento casi doblan a las francesas. Gracias a este magnífico esfuerzo, los aliados han podido reorganizarse, crear o reconstituir sus ejércitos, [illegible] de todos los medios modernos de combate...

Francia ha desempeñado con creces su parte en la tarea común. Y ¿no habrá llegado el momento de tenérselo en cuenta? ¿Será preciso que eche mano de sus últimos medios, en el momento en que, gracias a su energía, tantos otros pueden aligerarla de una parte de su pesada carga?

¿Cual es el país que, como el nuestro, se halla casi al extremo de sus recursos en hombres válidos? ¿Cuál es el que ha llamado a las filas los reclutas de 1888 y 1917 casi de niños y de ancianos? ¿A cuál le queda una población civil proporcionalmente tan poco numerosa?»

El articulista opina que, en vez de pedir más al pueblo que lo ha dado todo, es hora de devolverle los elementos inútilmente movilizados: sus heridos, sus enfermos, que gimen indefinidamente en los cuarteles, ambulancias y hospitales.

«¿Es que —pregunta— nuestra administración militar y nuestro gobierno no se dan cuenta de que, tras el ejército que combate, es preciso que el país trabaje, produzca, fabrique armamento, suministre víveres, pague impuestos y subscriba empréstitos? Y, ¿cómo es posible todo esto si no queda en los hogares ninguno de los elementos que aseguran en los tiempos normales la actividad y prosperidad nacionales?»

La perspectiva parécele impresionante al escritor francés y se preocupa en lo que será de su patria si queda suspendi-

Fig. 4.

Front page of *Diario de Gerona de avisos y noticias*, 5 April, 1916. Rafael Masó designed this heading for his father's newspaper in 1910. Fundació Rafael Masó Archive, reg. no. document 248.

City Council and member of the Provincial Corporation.

His first-born son, Santiago Masó, followed in his father's steps in the world of law and journalism. He graduated in law at the University of Barcelona in 1900 and got his doctorate in Madrid in 1903. He was a lawyer, a member of parliament in the Spanish Parliament for the Lliga Regionalista and led the *Diario de Gerona* after the death of his father. He stood out as a specialist in Catalan civil law and was appointed dean of the Lawyers Professional Association in 1936. He was also the first President of the Journalists Association of Girona, founded in 1914. From early on in his life Santiago Masó showed his political leaning, and while in his youth he formed part of the Joventut Catalanista de Girona, and in 1901 the Lliga Catalanista de Girona, founded that same year. In 1903 he was one of the founders in Girona of the Lliga Regionalista. He also had a leading role in 1909 in the opening in Girona of Caixa de Pensions per a la Vellesa i d'Estalvis savings bank. In 1918 he married Carme de Vinyals i de Font, and then bought the house at Ballesteries number 29, which became the single number for the four houses that Rafael Masó transformed into the current Casa Masó (fig. 5).

His brother Rafael was also supposed to continue living at the Masó House after his marriage to Esperança Bru, and that is why in the reform of the house in 1911 he had planned to use the first and second floors for his parents

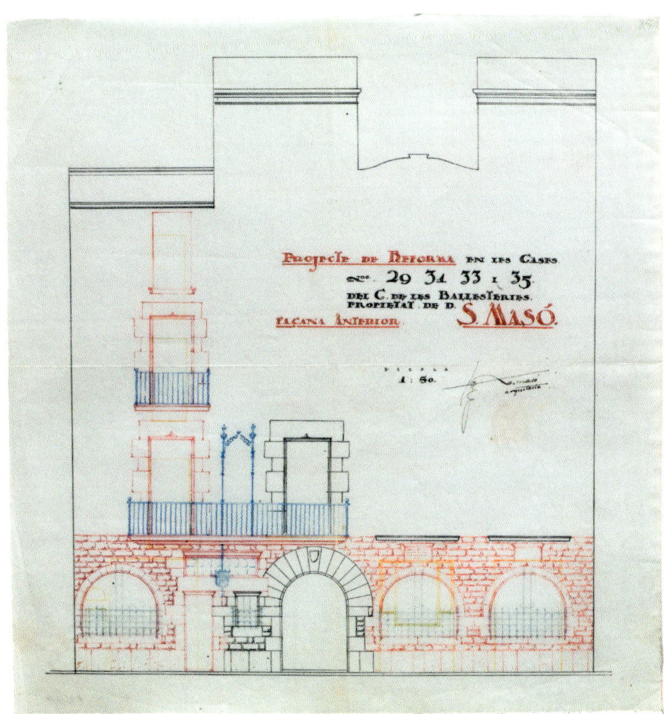

Fig. 5

Reform Project on Houses Numbers 29, 31, 33 and 35 of Ballesteries Street, property of Mr. S. Masó, 1918. Ink on paper, 40 x 38.2 cm. Historic Archive of the Col·legi d'Arquitectes de Catalunya – Demarcació de Girona, reg. no. 9517-9.

and brothers and sisters, and the third and fourth floors for him and his new family. But due to the demands of his father-in-law, who was against the marriage, the Masó Bru family ended up in another flat in Girona, at the beginning of Santa Eugènia Road, and there were born their seven children: Rosa, Francesc, Jordi, Rafael, Montserrat, Josep and Esperança.

Santiago Masó, therefore, inherited the entire property of Ballesteries Street, and with his wife, mother and sisters,

TODAS

occupied the first and second floors, while his brother Joan was the one who finally settled in the third floor. Joan Masó studied pharmacy and worked in the profession in the establishment at Argenteria Street that his brother Rafael had reformed in 1908. In 1915, on the death of his father, he went on to lead the family printing business. He also worked as a mathematics and Catalan teacher, even clandestinely. In 1924 he married Josefina Aragó Turon, from Santa Coloma de Farners. Joan Masó was very keen on hiking and photography, and his autochromes feature the first color photos that there are of Girona.[9] Narcís Masó, even though in 1912 he went to work in Terrassa, also continued living sporadically with his brothers and sisters in the Masó House until 1933, when he married Rosa Llunes. His work as a pedagogue represents the *noucentista* vocation for the modernization of education in Catalonia during the *Mancomunitat* and the Republic, above all with the creation of the Escola de S'Agaró.[10]

The women in the house

The role of the women in the Masó House was always decisive, but particularly in difficult times, such as during the Civil War. From their daily reality, inside the house, they made the family grow, helping the men of the house prosper in their life and professional projects, and were also fine partners in the family businesses. In this context, the mother of the family was in charge of the daily solving of domestic life as well as of the more spiritual aspect, which in the Masó home had a particular nuance. The atmosphere created by the Masó Valentí parents for their home reflected their love of traditions and special emphasis on the cultural, personal and spiritual education of their children. These values remained instilled in the minds

Fig. 6

Maria Masó, on the balcony of the Masó House, taking in the festival in Ballesteries Street, with a *cobla*, a Catalan tradiditonal music ensemble, in front of the house, c. 1915. Fundació Rafael Masó Archive, reg. image no. 135.

of the Masó children. The noucentista values of spirit of the home of the architect Rafael were in no way unusual, and nor were the attention to teaching the children by the pedagogue Narcís, and the love of work and commitment to the profession and the country of Joan and Santiago.

The dedication to the family and to the education of the children was experienced most intensely. For example, when Santiago, Rafael and Joan Masó went to study in Barcelona the deployment of a family logistics of provision and saving was necessary, controlled to a large extent by the family's mother, Paula Valentí.[11] The boys' careers were closely monitored from Ballesteries Street, where the exam dates were noted down on the calendar to wish them good luck in advance.[12]

The daughters went to classes for young ladies and were trained in domestic sciences to become wives and housewives. Of the three of them, only Maria de la Bonanova achieved this objective, and in 1920 married Estanislau Aragó, with whom she had three children: Montserrat, Anna Maria and Narcís-Jordi (fig. 6). Angelina and Paula Masó remained single and always lived in the house. Everything seemed to be going according to plan when the jolt of the Civil War put the family structure to the test and brought out the talent and strength of the women of the house.
The attacks and murder of highly representative people of the city meant that the men felt threatened and decided to leave. The Masó daughters and their sisters-in-law Josefina, Montserrat and Pilar Aragó remained in the house trying to run the family printers and struggling to survive with few resources. With their knowledge of embroidery and domestic work they organized a family workshop of making dolls and cloth figures and bags. They soon made contact with

Fig. 7

Collection of liturgical objects designed and made clandestinely by Paula Masó, 1936. Fundació Rafael Masó Archive, reg. no. 742-750.

the Santa Anna haberdashery in Barcelona and received orders for embroideries and baby clothes, which Paula Masó made. They also organized to get food, either through friends abroad who sent them packages, or via Foixà and other towns, where families they knew provided them with agricultural produce to survive.[13] Montserrat Aragó contributed to the family economy by organizing a tiny infant school of family friends in the Masó House.

After the war the Masó Valentí sisters continued showing their strengths. The eldest sister, Angelina, in her role as single aunt, was very important when taking care of the children and sick of the family. Maria de la Bonanova gave talks in Acció Catòlica, one of the few organizations that in post-war Catalonia offered possibilities of activity and commitment. Her sister Paula worked in the parish of Sant Feliu. Her status of being single made it possible for her to devote a lot of effort as organizer of the parish Catechism. She was known as "Miss Paula", and she was responsible for the organization of a parish school where she undertook an unquestionable role of social assistance among the children of the district, one of the most deprived in Girona at the time.[14] Paula was known in the family as "the one with fairy hands", referring to her great skill in making very delicate embroideries, often helped by her sister Angelina. This talent was greatly appreciated by the architect Rafael Masó, who commissioned her to produce many items for the house, as well as flags and standards for diverse organizations. Her skill also has an exceptional witness in a series of liturgical objects made during the war to attend to the clandestine catholic worship that took place in the Masó House (fig. 7).

Casa Masó was also home to some young men and women in domestic service, normally between one and three, according to the periods. Their work involved the daily shopping, washing, cleaning, ironing, serving and taking care of the children. For years their lives were completely linked to those of the masters of the house, and none of the many parties and celebrations or the majority of activities that took place in the house would have been possible without their work and dedication.

1 See Josep Canal *et al.*, *Atles d'història urbana segles VI a C-XVI* (Girona: Ajuntament / Institut Cartogràfic de Catalunya, 2010).

2 See "Información judicial recibida a Instrucción de los facultativos D. Francisco de Montaña, Dn. Pablo de Cortada y Dn. José Maria Steva residentes en esta ciudad," 1839. Fundació Rafael Masó Archive, reg. no. document 221.

3 A few years previously the Surgeons Association of Barcelona had been created, like those of the State. The document mentioned shows the vestiges of the old guild of barber-surgeons. See "Inventari firmat per lo Dn. Francisco Montaña Licenciat en Medicina i Cirurgia i en la present ciutat de Girona domiciliat,"16 September, 1833. Fundació Rafael Masó Archive, reg. no. document 219.

4 See the signed Will and Testament of Francesc de Paula Montaña, 12 July, 1870. Fundació Rafael Masó Archive, reg. no. document 207.

5 See Joan Ballart, "Els Masó, una família il·lustre d'americanos. Naviliers, escriptors, periodistes i arquitectes", *El Sot de l'Aubó* (2011): 21-25.

6 Masó House exhibits several paintings by Gaudenci Masó, among which feature the copies he made of the series dedicated to *Four Seasons* by Claudi Lorenzale (Palau de la Virreina, Barcelona).

7 The name of the newspaper changed three times and ended up as *Órgano del Partido de la Izquierda Liberal Dinástica de la Provincia de Gerona*. See "Nomenament de Gaudenci Masó com oficial de sala de l'Audiència," 29 January, 1890. Fundació Rafael Masó Archive, reg. no. document 2. On the date of the death of Gaudenci Masó, see *La Vanguardia*, 24 January, 1893.

8 The *Diari de Girona d'avisos i notícies*, by then in Catalan, was printed on the ground floor of the Masó House until the outbreak of the Civil War, in 1936, but the Masó printing press continued working until 1992. See Xavier Castillón, "L'Ajuntament de Girona ha comprat 323 boixos a la impremta Masó," *El Punt*, 22 July 1992, 24.

9 See Lluís-Esteve Casellas, ed., *Joan Masó i Valentí (1883-1973): fotos* (Girona: Ajuntament, 1994).

10 See Salomó Marquès, *Narcís Masó, pedagog de l'escola activa* (Girona: Diputació, 1990).

11 These activities are documented in the extensive correspondence exchanged between parents and children, where each family member has their own leading role, either with encouragement for exams, consolation for the results or organising the administration. See Letter from Paula Valentí to Santiago Masó, c. 1894. Fundació Rafael Masó Archive, reg. no. document 336.

12 See, for example, "Val per un projectat coixí d'estil alemany que no s'ha pogut portar a cap a conseqüència d'haver passat massas hores fent novenes per l'èxit dels exàmens," undated. Fundació Rafael Masó Archive, reg. no. document 1.129; and Letter from Rafael Masó Pagès, from Paula Valentí and from all the sisters to Santiago Masó, congratulating him on having completed the last exam in his lawyer's degree, 14 November, 1900. Fundació Rafael Masó Archive, reg. no. document 438.

13 See the Letter from Cyprien Puig to Angelina Masó, where he describes the package he has sent to the Masó family from Montpellier, 25 November, 1938. Fundació Rafael Masó Archive, document 1.141. The hazardous circumstances of the Civil War are documented in the diary of Maria de la Bonanova Masó and Montserrat Aragó Masó, in which they recount the day to day life in the house. Fundació Rafael Masó Archive, reg. no. document 2.757.

14 Her pedagogic leaning led her to compile a series of popular children's songs, which she later taught to the children. See Songs transcribed by Paula Masó, 1912. Fundació Rafael Masó Archive, reg. no. document 1.149.

Living in Casa Masó

Narcís-Jordi Aragó Masó

I was just four years old when I went to live at the Masó House. I spent the whole three years of the Civil War. There, with the help of my sister Montserrat, I learnt to read and write in the language of my parents. There I tasted the bitterness of precarious food and heard the howling of the sirens warning of the bombardments (fig. 1). I was the only male inhabitant of a house full of women: my mother, my two sisters, my two Masó aunts, my three Aragó aunts and three maids. The men of the family, pursued by revolutionary bands from July 1936, had hidden in Barcelona or had crossed the French border clandestinely, and would not return until the end of the conflict. Then, with my father happily found again, the Aragó Masó family would return to our normal home in Ciutadans Street, in the very high second floor of the Gothic palace of the Salieti family that Uncle Rafael had restored from top to bottom (fig. 2).

From then on, and for many years, we only went to the Masó home now and then: to visit the uncles and aunts on Sunday afternoons or to congratulate them on their saint's day. We often coincided with the Masó Bru or Masó Llunes cousins. We youngsters, settled in the gallery, built big buildings with a marvellous architecture game so rich in columns, arches, tympanums and rectangular blocks of stone of all colours and sizes like I have never seen anywhere again. If we went into the kitchen, we were looked after maternally by the maids: the old cook had had us all on her lap since we were very little and she loved us like a

Fig. 1

Narcís-Jordi Aragó in the pergola of the Masó House, 1937. Photographer unknown.

grandmother. The waitress, younger, wore an impeccable white apron, an obligatory uniform when serving dinner or afternoon tea. On Saint James's Day we ate all together in the dining room on the first floor, which Uncle Rafael had conceived as the family sanctuary. In mid-afternoon, the sun, tinged by the coloured stained glass windows, winked from the gallery and projected onto the wall the moving reflection of the river. For Saint John's Day, we went up to the third floor, where Aunt Josefina served us with an ingenuous euphoria the best custard in the world.

Uncles and aunts: the latter years

This is how I saw the life of the inhabitants of the Masó home flow until their end. The first to leave was Aunt Carme de Vinyals, at 54. I was 11 and had never seen anyone dead close up; neither had I seen Uncle Santiago cry as he did that day. After that, Aunt Paula and Aunt Angelina, like two angels sent from heaven, took care of their older sister. The three of them lived on the first and second floors of the family home, where they had been born and where they had always lived.

On the third floor, planned initially by Rafael Masó as his own home, lived Joan Masó and Josefina Aragó, my double uncle and aunt, on my mother's and father's side (fig. 3). Also living there intermittently was Aunt Montserrat Aragó, librarian of the Caixa de Pensions savings bank with diverse destinations. Visiting Uncle Joan, cordial and extremely warm, meant enjoying his collection of exotic minerals, the unending series of stereoscopic photographs or the half dozen singular and exclusive children's toys. When he left the printing works to his workers in exchange for a discrete life pension, he devoted his time to

Fig. 2

Maria de la B. Masó and Estanislau Aragó with their children. From left to right, Anna M., Narcís-Jordi and Montserrat, April 1939. Photograpph by Joan Masó.

Fig. 3

Joan Masó and Josefina Aragó, 1941. Photographer unknown.

teaching Catalan, to translating texts from the German that he had mysteriously taught himself, by listening to foreign radio stations and maintaining contact in writing and in person with friends from his youth, exiled or returned to Girona, of an ideology that did not always coincide with his own. He lived for 90 years with all his faculties and curiosities.

On the fourth floor, in the first post-war years, in refuge was Uncle Narcís, with Aunt Rosa and the children, Mercè and Ricard. He survived thanks to private classes and decoration work, often inspired by the style of his brother Rafael. He channelled his pedagogic and social concerns with the creation of the Apprentice School, sponsored by Acció Catòlica and the Bishopric.

Uncle Santiago, the heir, the central figure of the family, was the typical example of the "defeated winners" of the Civil War: the Francoist dictatorship completely dried up his political career (fig. 4). He spent thirty years without any other public activity than that of Acció Catòlica, of which he was the diocesan president, nor any other job than a lawyer, with good clients such as the Grober factory, the L. Mata i Pons company, Energia Elèctrica de Catalunya, Aigües de Girona, the railway companies of Sant Feliu de Guíxols and Olot, the writer Caterina Albert... He had two successive articled clerks: Manuel Teixidor Comes, brother of the poet and publisher Joan Teixidor, and Joan B. Muntada

Macau, lawyer and poet. He corresponded with old friends such as Vallès i Pujals, Ventosa i Calvell, Trias de Bes, Pi i Sunyer, Gual Villalbí, Millet Maristany or Ramon d'Abadal, with the public notaries Adroer and Porcioles and with the architects Benavent, Danés and Giralt.[1] He was dean of the Lawyers' Association, but the Spanish government, aware of his lack of support for the Regime, did not want to award him the Cross of Sant Raimon de Penyafort that his colleagues had requested for him, and was awarded a distinction of a lower ranking: the Gold Medal of Merit in Justice. More than one thousand volumes of his collection of legal books have been incorporated into the library of the Universitat de Girona, while the writings corresponding to his work as a jurist are deposited in 71 bundles in the Historic Archive of the Girona City Council.[2]

Fig. 4

Santiago Masó and Carme Vinyals, c. 1941. Photographer unknown.

Half a century in the family home

Due to his status as registered heir, Uncle Santiago had to pass on the inheritance to the oldest brother or sister with children. This is how the Masó House came to be the property of my mother, Maria de la Bonanova, married to Estanislau Aragó, teacher, journalist and court attorney. When my uncle died, in 1960, aged 82, we left the house in Ciutadans Street to settle in the new home. This was my "Return to Brideshead". One year later, Mercè Huerta Busquets became my wife and would form part of the nucleus of the inhabitants of the house (fig. 5).

Fig. 5

Mercè Huerta in the gallery of the Masó House, 1987. Photograph by Narcís-Jordi Aragó.

The first surprise of the new house was that of the silence. We discovered that what flowed near the galleries created a static space of absolute quiet, totally removed from the bustle of the street. Margarita Colom, in a poem, imagined the Masó House "sailing between silences like a mythical ship." [3] The Onyar River slipped slowly past amid curtains of mist, crossed by the parallel lines of the bridges over which a thousand figures crossed back and forth repeated in the mirror of the water. We saw how the city came and went with an incessant flow, while the river passed by, implacable like the passing of time. The only sound that accompanied us was that of the printing machines that occupied the entire ground floor of the building. Every morning, from bed, we heard them cradled by their rhythmic song: a measured toing and froing that made the beams creak gently and produced vibrations of glass in the windows

Fig. 6

The River Onyar on a rainy day, from the Masó House, 2006. Photograph by Narcís-Jordi Aragó.

and balconies. The smell of fresh ink climbed up the stairs and filtered, balsamically, beneath the doors of all the rooms.

The second surprise, inexhaustible, was that of touching the furniture, moving the chests of drawers, opening the drawers and finding the uncountable vestiges of the life lived as a result of successive inheritances; oil paintings, engravings, silver candelabras, silk fans, jars, flower vases, fruit bowls, trays, porcelain crockery, silver cutlery, glass cups, towels and linen sheets, damask bedcovers... as well as hundreds of books, magazines, photographs, documents, letters, newspaper cuttings, prints... In the Masó home they never threw anything out, and we also agreed that we had to keep everything. Mercè, as a painter especially sensitive towards the world of art, knew how to value these domestic treasures exactly and they

Fig. 7

Family meal at the Masó House, 2007.
Photographer unknown.

were saved through fiercely resisting the siege of antique collectors and offers from second-hand dealers.

Therefore, we always lived in the shadow of our ancestors; every day we came across over and again the stamp of their past in all the corners of the house which, as Rafael Masó had written, had the walls "all touched with love and florid with desires." [4] She had enriched everything with her emotive and affective deepness and with the capacity she had of transforming any moment of coexistence into a renewed source of art and beauty. Everything responded, as Eva Vàzquez said, "to a determination to celebrate the miniscule home life, so important in the details, in the daily trifles." [5]

The architect Joan Roca Pinet and the surveyor and interior designer Ferran Ventós made the minimum essential reforms to the property to facilitate the half-shared lives of both couples: the parents, on the first floor, and the children, on the second floor. I settled in the lawyer's office of Uncle Santiago and Mercè set up the painting studio in the old servants' rooms, on the third floor, accessible via an interior spiral staircase. My father improvised an attorney's office in the living room: there he regularly received the unending clientele of tenant farmers, farmworkers and artisans who came to solve their problems. Also retired from all political activity, the former councilor for culture of the City Council was diocesan vice-president of the men of Acció Catòlica. His colleagues repeatedly chose him as dean of the Attorneys' Association, and he did, on completing fifty years activity in the profession, receive the first-class distinguished Cross of Sant Raimon de Penyafort, awarded personally by the Minister of Justice.

In those years we shared with our parents the anguish of the last Girona floods, awoken during the night by the screams of the sirens and the exalted cries of the neighbors. The Onyar flowed downstream dense and crazy; it lapped against the ground floors of the houses and entered through the windows of the basements while the shopkeepers prepared to take the stock to the loft or the floor above (fig. 6).

From private home to public asset

When my father and mother died, aged 86 and 89 respectively, Mercè and I remained alone on the two floors of the house. We tried to establish a subtle balance between the inherited treasure and the personal belongings added. We maintained the tradition of the family festival feasts (fig. 7), of the meetings with friends who were writers, artists and activists, and the more or less clandestine meetings with journalists and politicians. The Masó House was, throughout the last half century, that which it had always been, from the distant times of the Lliga Regionalista or of the Floral Games poetry competitions: the setting for many concerns and the melting pot of many civic initiatives. Our happy stay in the house connected perfectly with the fruitful period featuring parents, aunts and grandparents.

This is why we believed, finally, that the building, with all it contained, could not be just for us: it had to lose its private nature to become an asset of public interest and use. So, on the 7 April 2006 —the one-hundredth anniversary of the day on which Rafael Masó graduated as an architect— we ceded the property and its assets to Girona City Council so that it would become, through a foundation, a not-to-be-missed piece of architectural and cultural historic heritage of the city (fig. 8).

Fig. 8

The Mayoress of Girona, Anna Pagans, with the Aragó Huerta couple in the act of ceding the Masó House to Girona City Council, 2006. Photograph by Josep M. Oliveras.

1 See Epistolary of Santiago Masó Valentí, Fundació Rafael Masó Archive.

2 See "El Fons Antecessores," UdG Library, Special collections, consulted 7 January 2012, http://www.udg.edu/biblioteca/Fonsespecials/FonsAntecessores/tabid/12033/language/ca-ES/Default.aspx; and "Fons Santiago Masó," in Ramon Alberch, *Guia Inventari de l'Arxiu Històric de l'Ajuntament de Girona* (Girona: Servei Municipal de Publicacions, 1983), 128.

3 Margarita Colom, "Sé d'un indret a Girona," in Colom, *Girona, ciutat submergida* (Girona: Llibres del segle, 1995), 74.

4 Rafael Masó, "De les èglogues del novell arquitecte," in *Masó, Antologia poètica*, ed. David Prats (Girona: Fundació Valvi / CCG Edicions, 2000), 59.

5 Eva Vàzquez, "Cases amb protagonista: la Casa Masó de Girona," *Revista de Girona* no. 183 (July-August 1997): 100.

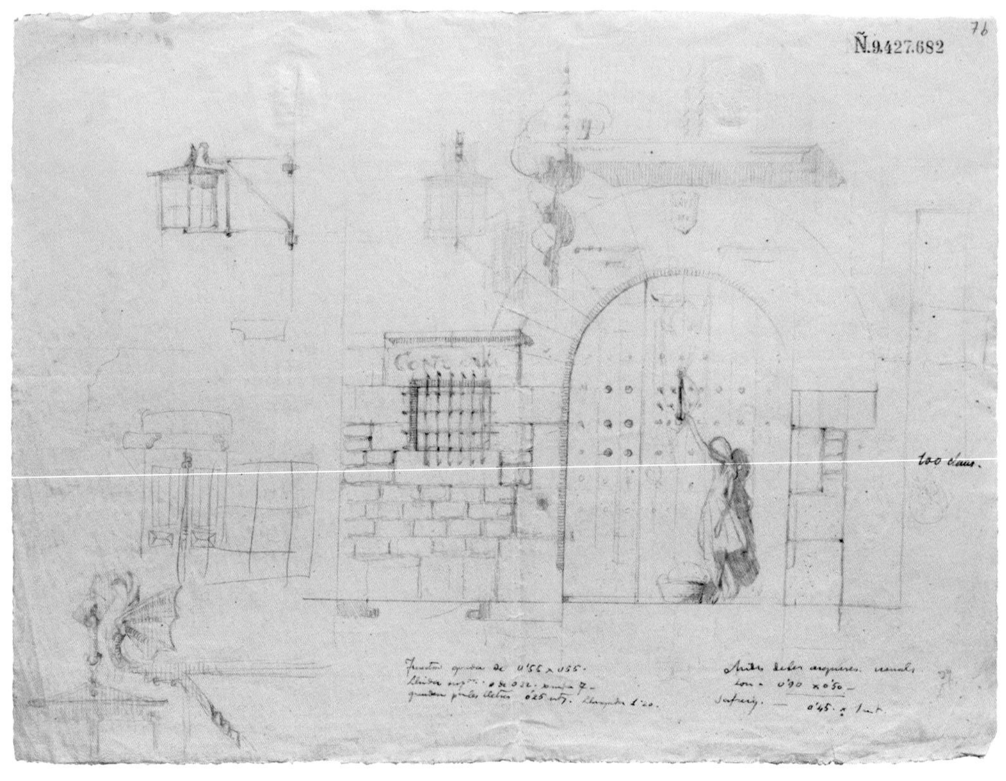

Fig. 1

Reform of the Masó House, Elevation of Ballesteries Street Portal, c. 1910. Pencil and ink on paper, 32 x 43.5 cm. Historic Archive of the Col·legi d'Arquitectes de Catalunya – Demarcació de Girona, reg. no. 9517-12.

The *noucentista* home: the work of Rafael Masó in the Casa Masó

Jordi Falgàs

Architects from Girona … have blown their noses on German magazines and go about sticking strange and horrible blobs all over the city.

—

Josep Pla, *Girona*, 1952[1]

Rafael Masó felt a true devotion to the house he was born in, and before becoming an architect he made it appear in his poetic work.[2] In 1905 he published "*El plaent dematí en la meva cambra*" (The placid morning in my room); in 1906 he did a full tour of the building in verse, from the street to the roof, in "*De les èglogues del novell arquitecte*" (On the eclogues of the new architect); in 1907 he dedicated one of the two compositions in "*El llibre del retorn*" (The book of return) to the house; and his contribution in the *Almanach dels noucentistes*, in 1911, was the poem "*De la llar*" (Of the home).[3] In the second poem, six years still before his marriage to Esperança Bru, he already showed his intention of reforming the house and going to live there with "the children that would come and the wife I must marry." [4] The identification between the house and the object of his amorous desire is so much that the poet saw anthropomorphic qualities in the building and presaged that it would become something "splendid like the woman I love / and you will take her gesture and so sublime poses." [5] Finally, at the demand of the bride's father, the Masó Bru couple were unable to live in the building in Ballesteries Street, but until 1912 the reforms and objects that the architect designed were undertaken

with the conviction that that house would be the home of his new family, on the third and fourth floors; over those of his parents and brothers and sisters, who occupied the first and second. As such, the exterior and the interiors had to be the best reflection of his way of understanding architecture and, in consequence, of his personal and collective values and ideals.

This first stage of works by Masó for the family house began with the design of a series of objects for the home in 1909, and culminated in 1912 after more than one year of reforms of openings and of heights of the facade, and of unifying the interiors of number 31 with numbers 33 and 35.[6] On the young couple not being able to live there, the third floor was reformed (for example, the gallery facing the street and which is dated 1912, or the small windows on what would have been the architect's studio) but the interiors remained as they were (after some years the glass windows of the dining room were placed) and the furniture that had already been made had to be adapted to their new home in another flat in Girona.

Fig. 2

Reform of the Masó House, Sketch of Ballesteries Street Entrance, c. 1910. Pencil and watercolor on paper, 13.5 x 21 cm. Historic Archive of the Col·legi d'Arquitectes de Catalunya – Demarcació de Girona, reg. no. 9517-24.

The second stage of interventions by Masó on the house of his birth began in 1916, after the death of his father, and above all in 1918, when his elder brother, Santiago, married and occupied the first and second floors, in which he

Fig. 3

Vestibule of the first floor and interior staircase of the Masó House, 1911. Photograph from 1916. Fundació Institut Amatller d'Art Hispànic, Arxiu Mas, Barcelona.

lived with his mother and sisters, and his brother Joan moved in to the third floor. Santiago, who was already a leading lawyer and politician, commissioned him with a new reform of the facades, both in Ballesteries Street and that of the river, at the same time as he bought a fourth adjoining house (number 29), which was also added to the others, with the resulting creation of new interior spaces on all the floors and of the corresponding furnishings, windows and other ornaments. The structure and appearance that is conserved until today is, essentially, that which was completed in 1919.

Unlike when he worked for his clients —with whom he often had disagreements about the projects—, when Masó conceived the reform of the house of his birth he always did it thinking about himself or his family, and therefore each intervention was an opportunity to create and present an image of himself and those around him. In this sense, the work of Rafael Masó at the Masó House is a small anthology of his contribution to the language of architecture and interior design, since here he could work without fear of rejection and endeavoring to make reality that which he and his generation held as ideal. And as *noucentista*, in the Girona of the early 20th century it was essential to generate a specific image of modernity strongly anchored to mythical narrations of the historical and cultural tradition of Catalonia.

Interiors resistant to exterior storms

In the 1930s, Walter Benjamin already described how since the 19th century the new urban bourgeoisie gave the interior of their homes prime importance in order to project a modern image, and the individual conceived interior decoration as a "casing" loyal to his impression.[7] In *noucentista* Catalonia, and above all in light of the outbreaks of working class violence that threatened the bourgeois status, just as had occurred in the 1909 Tragic Week, the writers Eugeni d'Ors and Joaquim Folch i Torres dedicated numerous articles to describing what the ideal home should be like, with the twofold intention of creating a model for the bourgeoisie and that at the same time they would impose it on the working class.

In this climate, in the column entitled "*La felicitat*" (Happiness), Eugeni d'Ors described his ideal interior in terms that reveal the values underlying the architectonic, decorative, aesthetic and social model that he advocated:

> Happiness ... consists of living a quiet and busy life within a few rooms, two or three, where there are various windows and many nooks. The windowpanes should be covered with little white curtains, of medium transparency, because excessive opacity would dim the light and too much translucidity would take away privacy. The nooks should be filled in a profound and subtle way. It is a good idea to place paintings, etchings, books, statuettes, simple and definitive vases holding flowers and leaves where the plants have taken on a perennial nature and the admirable repose of inert mineral things. The aim that needs to be achieved is... that the nooks that your eyes contemplate each day can be, nevertheless, reaching a specific day, a specific moment, appear to you so unusual it was as if

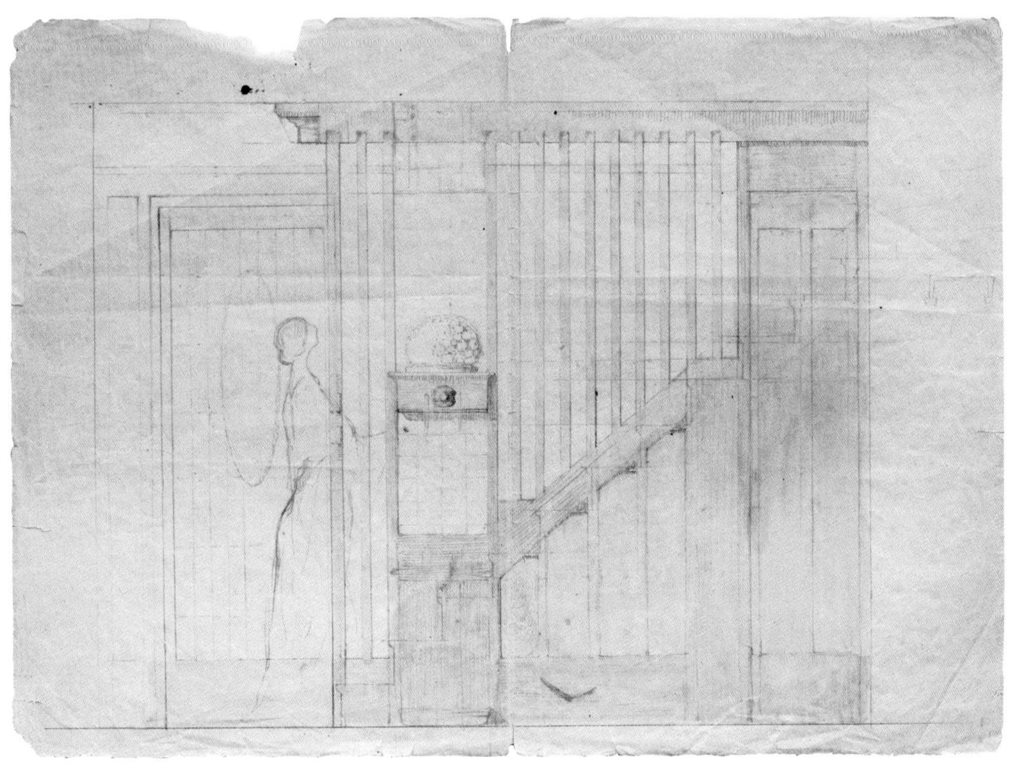

Fig. 4

Reform of the Masó House, Elevation of the Interior Staircase Between the Third and Fourth Floors, 1910, not undertaken. Pencil and watercolor on paper, 32.5 x 45 cm. Historic Archive of the Col·legi d'Arquitectes de Catalunya – Demarcació de Girona, reg. no. 9517-40.

you were seeing them for the first time: here you have the rock upon which your interior peace and your joie de vivre may be built, secure from external storms ... There are in Barcelona artists capable of making a Cathedral and incapable of imagining a small interior like this.[8]

Ors again took advantage of the opportunity to criticize the artist capable of making a cathedral —that is, Antoni Gaudí— who for him represented all the ornamental

Fig. 5.

View of the dining room, with the lamp from 1910 and the desk from 1919. Photograph by Joan Masó, 1923. Centre de Recerca i Difusió de la Imatge, Ajuntament de Girona, reg. no. 25623.

excesses of *Modernisme*. Instead, he defended a new model of interior design based on austerity and simplicity, able to provide "happiness and interior peace" precisely because it was designed to withstand the "storms" that could threaten the property of the middle class.

The ideological convergence of Masó with Ors and Folch i Torres was such that the former lamented, in the following terms, being unable to send Folch the project for the interior decoration of his future apartment in the Masó House:

> Oh yes! It shall be well done and well drawn, and more than done and drawn, completed in everything of our

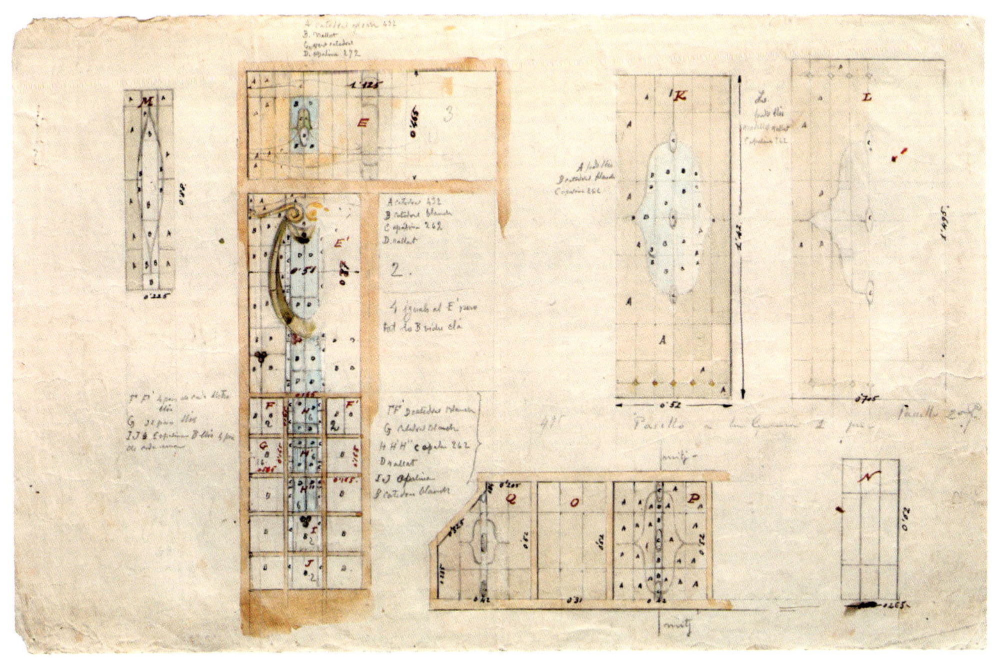

> house... I will send it to you because it shall indeed be worthy and adapted to that sensibility sought by Folch by me and by every thinking person that the arts in our land must take... Oh yes! Our rooms, our little nest, will have that Catalan flavor that he so desires and that he finds almost nowhere in what is being done.[9]

Fig. 6

Design for the Dining Room Windows and Other Stained-glass Windows of the Masó House, c. 1918. Pencil, ink and watercolor on paper, 28 x 44.2 cm. Historic Archive of the Col·legi d'Arquitectes de Catalunya – Demarcació de Girona, reg. no. 9517-49.

Masó worked on the project during all of 1910, and sketched some furniture as the work progressed, from May 10, 1910 until the couple had returned from their honeymoon at the end of March or in April of 1912. Just as Tarrús and Comadira have observed, the willingness to adapt modern solutions to an old and traditional past is what led Rafael Masó to use a

Fig. 7

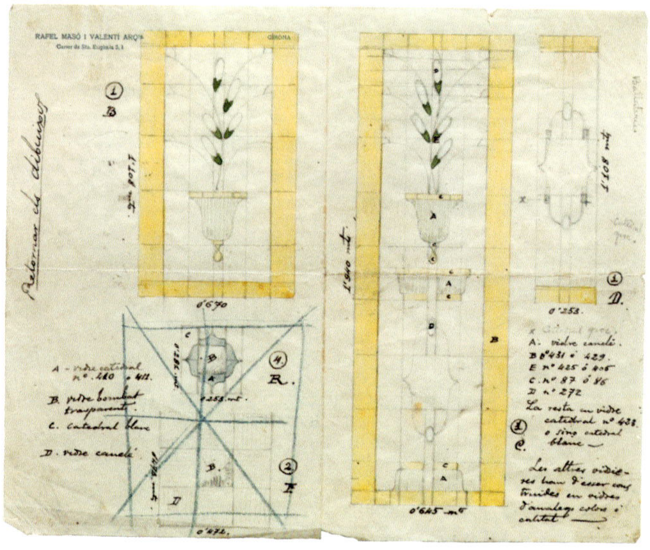

Design for the Bathroom Windows and Others on the Second Floor of the Masó House, Girona, c. 1918. Paper, ink and watercolor on paper, 22 x 27 cm. Historic Archive of the Col·legi d'Arquitectes de Catalunya – Demarcació de Girona, reg. no. 9517-55.

series of elements from the medieval and baroque traditions evident in buildings close to the Masó House in Girona.[10] This desire responded to the fact that the Masó family had attained a new social status and, above all, a significant public presence in the turn-of-the-century Girona. Now that they were influential and well known among the bourgeoisie of the city, they wanted a house that would symbolize their desire to be rooted in the medieval past of the city and of the neighborhood where they lived, and their commitment to modernity and progress via a certain degree of luxury and comfort.

Masó achieved the appearance of an old family seat with blocks of rough-faced stone on the lower part of the facade, a round arch entryway, characteristic of country houses and Gothic buildings, and an entrance with a second round

Fig. 8

Embroidery Design for the Lampshade of the Dining Room Lamp at the Masó House, 1915. Pencil and watercolor on paper, 16 x 20.5 cm. Historic Archive of the Col·legi d'Arquitectes de Catalunya – Demarcació de Girona, reg. no. 9517-93.

arch, exposed wood beams, and ceramic and wrought-iron elements of medieval and popular inspiration (fig. 1). For the wall covering of the stairway, for example, he designed nineteen small ceramic tiles, and for each one invented a different heraldic motif related to the surnames and occupations of his grandparents, parents and siblings. In the entrance, creating a strong chromatic contrast, he used the traditional square tile in green and white, which had also been frequent in vernacular Catalan for centuries (fig. 2).

The solid and aged aspect of the facade and entrance changes on entering the vestibule of the first floor, where the dimensions and the decoration of the spaces are those of a modern home that does not renounce the vernacular aftertaste. Masó based his work on the combination of materials befitting the large Catalan farmhouses, symbols of tradition:

wood, stained glass, decorative metal and glazed ceramics. The interior baseboards and wainscots were covered with various pieces of ceramic designed by the architect, all in straw and caramel colors. In the interior stairway that leads to the second floor, bathed by natural light filtered through a skylight, the panelling is glazed ceramic, and in the inner part Masó used a resource frequent to the interiors of Voysey and Mackintosh —for example Broadleys, The Orchard, the Hill House and the Willow Tea Room— consistent in creating a floor-to-ceiling wall formed by narrow, elongated wooden slats, with an empty space between them (fig. 3). Masó had also planned to repeat the same solution on the inner stairway that had to join the third and fourth floor (fig. 4), and he used it in the inner stairway of the homes of the Teixidor Flour Mill, the Masramon House, the Casas House, and the Ensesa House. This solution enabled him to create verticality and dynamism of empty and full volumes, since the light from the skylight caused a play of contrasts between the dark tonality of the wood and the straw colour of the ceramic, which gives the space a sensation of depth and height that it would not otherwise possess.

In the dining room, above the baseboard, Masó covered the walls with bands of thin wicker up to a height of two meters, finishing them with a dark wooden ledge that stood out against the background and ran all around the room, used to display small sculptures and decorative objects (fig. 5). The upper part of the walls was a space for hanging paintings, and the ceiling was coffered with plaster painted to imitate wood. The dining room chairs, of turned wood and the backs in latticed palm cord, were of a type deriving from popular Catalan furnishing.[11] For the dining room doors he designed stained-glass windows with stylized campanulas and garlands that allowed him to introduce a simple note of

colour (fig. 6). The geometric stylization of a flower and the combination and repetition of the drawing to be able to apply it on different surfaces and materials (textiles, painted paper, stained-glass windows, stencil) was also a common decorative resource in the interiors of Mackintosh, Baillie Scott and Josef Hoffmann, among others. In the Masó House, the stylized flowers appear in other glass windows of doors and interior openings, the most outstanding of which is the double window of the second-floor bathroom (fig. 7).

The object that Masó designed expressly for the dining room was a large hanging lamp of wrought iron, copper and colored glass, in which he tried to combine the medieval look and the popular character of manual ironwork with the modernity of rectilinear shapes and geometric volumes. Contrasting with the hardness of metal, Masó designed a silk flounce that served as a shade. The first one installed had the light of the Holy Ghost as motif, but after just a few years it was replaced by a design that insisted on the motif of the campanulas (fig. 8). Along with the rose (which appears in some stained-glass windows of a first-floor room), the motif of the stylized bellflower is one of the most frequent in the work of the Wiener Werkstätte. It is present not only in architecture, in latticed windows and wall decoration, but also in silverware and jewelry, stained-glasswork and textiles, and indeed in practically all the products of the era, both in the work of Hoffmann as in that of other artists from the Werkstätte. For Masó, as for the Austrian artists, the bellflower not only served to symboli-

Fig. 9

View of the first floor gallery with flower boxes designed by Rafael Masó, c. 1912. Photo by Adolf Mas, 1916, Fundació Institut Amatller d'Art Hispànic, Arxiu Mas, Barcelona.

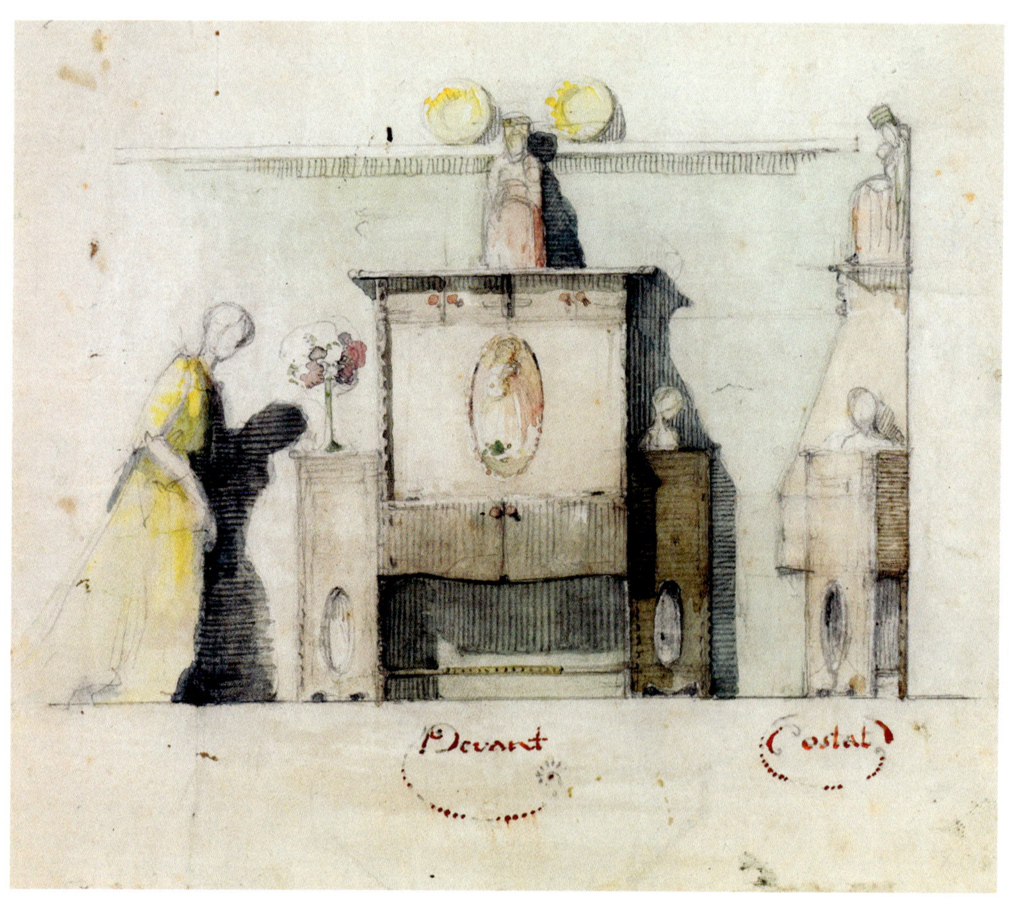

Fig. 10

Front and Side Elevation of the Desk for Esperança Bru, 1910. Pencil, ink and watercolour on paper, 17.8 x 20.9 cm. Joan Tarrús Collection, Barcelona.

cally introduce nature into their interiors, it also served to represent the simplicity, delicacy and purity of their work. The inverted chalice shape also allowed for multiple combinations of geometry and color that could be reproduced with various materials and techniques. As well as using it in his house, Masó also introduced it in the Masramon, Ensesa and Casas houses.

For the gallery, Masó designed two wooden flower boxes, painted white with dark vertical rectangular strips, which fitted into a rectangular-based metallic support with four legs (fig. 9). The decoration of the metal plate is a grid of small holes arranged geometrically, abstract and simple, and similar to the *Gitterwerke* (lattice work) used by Hoffmann and Koloman Moser during the early years of the Werkstätte to design a series of objects characterized by the metal grid. The whole was an interior dominated by the art and crafts ethos, in which both the natural light of the gallery and the artificial light were filtered and shaded by stained glass windows and curtains with the aim of creating the point of sophistication and modernity in balance with the sobriety of the materials of vernacular origin. Once again, the model of simplicity, austerity and refinement followed the precepts of Ors and Folch in every way.

The interior that was not

The furnishings for his future house on the third and fourth floors of the Masó House are what the architect would have wanted to have drawn to send to Folch i Torres and show him up to what point he personified the ideals of the *noucentista* home.[12] Between 1910 and 1911 Masó designed and commissioned the construction of the furniture for the bedroom (desk, wardrobe and bed – figs.

10 and 11), and the furniture for the living room (table, chairs, armchairs, buffet and cupboard – fig. 12) he drew in May 1911 and did not finish until March 1912, when he personally brought from Germany the curved glass windows for the desk and sideboard.[13] This long process—indirectly caused by the opposition to the marriage of the bride's father—allowed Masó to create two homogeneous sets and to make every detail count. As he explains in his letters, he devoted considerable effort to the limited but significant symbolic elements of the furniture. The majority of them were religious, for example, the image inside the desk of the Virgin of Hope (*Esperança*), or the terracotta relief on the bed's headboard of the biblical scene of Jacob's Ladder.

The design of both sets of furniture is based on regularly-shaped planes, much more than for anything he had designed before, with rectilinear outlines, smooth surfaces, symmetrical composition and minimal ornamentation. Masó used a geometric shape to give unity to each set: the oval (which he would begin to use in his buildings) in the bedroom, and the square in the dining room. On the chairs, he created a simple but effective abstract motif with a beveled quadrangle, which subtly breaks the horizontality of the back and gives it a three-dimensional effect, since beveled wood always reflects light from one of its surfaces. On the buffet and the cupboard he played with bevels, the cavities of the doors and the drawers, and a series of squares and concentric circles over vertical or inclined planes, ornamented only with a double edging of round head bolts made of wood. At the same time, the modernity of the geometric design coexists with the conscious introduction of rustic and vernacular elements, such as the curtains and the seats of woven jute.

Fig. 11

Perspective of the Bed and Wardrobe for the Masó Bru Apartment, 1910. Ink and watercolour on cardboard, 25.5 x 35.5 cm. Joan Tarrús Collection, Barcelona.

Masó did not conceal that many of his ideas and models came from English architects and furniture designers. In a letter in which he describes the design of the wardrobe, he explains that the design comes from "the English, who have created a kind of double wardrobe which is what I've adopted for our future marriage chamber."[14] Features such as the broad, horizontal overhang of the top, and the unadorned solid wood surfaces were common in the simplified cottage furniture designed by Voysey, Baillie Scott, E. A. Taylor, and John Ednie, among others, for manufacturers and retailers like London's Liberty & Co., Heal & Son, John P. White's Pyghtle Works in Bedford, and Glasgow's Wylie & Lochhead. Beyond the formal similarities, as Tarrús and Comadira point out, what Masó had found in the character of English domesticity was the moral significance of interiors, and in that too he agreed with Ors and Folch. Speaking of his plans for the nuptial chamber, he said in the same letter:

> Everything is of an austere and temperate color, walls, furniture, fabric, everything! And in everything there is perfect proportion and equilibrium... All of the furniture is of the same height. This is true of the openings as well. Everything ends in a line, and there is not a dissonant note of shape or of color bc everything blends into the same range of severe and distinguished colors ... There is nothing to distress the spirit but rather everything helps to concentrate it + and who knows why everything exudes a sweetness that reaches the soul ... How different from what one usually sees and how different from what the famous "bridal suite" usually consists of ... Ostentation and nothing + than ostentation! ... Oh, yes! Dissipation, banality, frivolity, superficiality... all of this is present in those rooms arranged in the modern style (meaning that this modernity is of the year two) ... So it is that while starting to live in a room like this it must seem that from then on life should become + sincere and + thoughtful, + true and + restful, beginning to live in the other kind of room must produce quite the opposite effect ... [for the bride] begins a life of pretense and dissipation, an artificial life, ostentatious, completely frivolous and completely empty like that very furniture and with that same atmosphere that is sensed in their nuptial chamber.[15]

Fig. 12

Furniture for the dining room of the Masó Bru apartment, 1911. Made by Miquel Pratmans. Chestnut wood, glass, metallic applications and palm cord. Coralí Gilabert Masó Collection, Girona.

This testimony indicates that Masó was conscious of the meaning of the aesthetic change that he and his generation were putting into practice less than a decade after what he called "modernity of the year two." It also shows how he shared the belief expressed by Folch that the furniture and decoration were carriers of ideas and moral values that had a direct effect on their users. The Masó House today features different series of furnishings that the architect designed at the commission of his brothers Santiago and Joan, some years later, when they occupied different parts of the house. For Santiago he designed the dining room cupboard and sideboard, a table and a bookcase for his lawyer's office; and for Joan's bedroom, a set of bed, wardrobe and dressing table.

Unlike Ors, the question to which Folch i Torres must have devoted more pages was that of the need for vernacular architecture to be the basis for the founding of a modern national architecture, a subject that is either in the background or the core of the majority of his articles from 1911 to 1913. During these years he undertook a periodic monitoring of the work "of the most eminent young architects from the Catalan school," who were for him above all Josep Goday, Rafael Masó and Josep M. Pericas.[16] Folch made known his approach to writing on architecture and on all of the arts related to it—furniture, interior decoration, the decorative arts, the restoration of monuments, and the recuperation of artistic crafts— with the desire to show that in Catalonia, unlike the rest of Spain, conditions were ripe for what was already happening in other places in Europe, especially in young nations like Germany and Italy.[17] For Folch and for Masó, art and architecture were essential components of nation-building, and as such they had to share certain identifying traits, just as their creators could not turn their backs on their nationality. This *Heimatschutzstil* was, moreover, a necessary condition for modern art.

1 Josep Pla, *Girona: un llibre de records* (Barcelona: Destino, 1998), 50-51.

2 This article includes fragments from my doctoral dissertation. See Jordi Falgàs, "Modernity and Tradition in Catalan Noucentisme: Rafael Masó's Regionalist Architecture, 1911-1917" (PhD diss., University of Wisconsin-Madison, 2011).

3 Rafael Masó, *Antologia poètica*, ed. David Prats (Girona: Fundació Valvi, 2006), 37, 51-52, 57-60, 74.

4 Ibid., 59.

5 Ibid.

6 For a more detailed chronology of all the works, see Joan Tarrús and Narcís Comadira, *Rafael Masó: arquitecte noucentista* (Girona: Brau / Col·legi d'Arquitectes de Catalunya, 2007, 2nd ed.), 262-63; and Jordi Bosch and Joan Tarrús, "Pla director de la seu de la Fundació Rafael Masó. Memòria," *La Punxa* no. 53 (2012): 14-25. I would like to thank Rosa M. Gil for her research to confirm the dating of the different reforms.

7 Walter Benjamin, *The Arcades Project*, ed. Rolf Tiedemann, trans. Howard Eiland and Kevin McLaughlin (Cambridge, Mass.: Belknap Press of Harvard University Press, 2003), 220. About the modern interior, see Penny Sparke, *The Modern Interior* (London: Reaktion Books, 2008), and Penny Sparke *et al.*, ed., *Designing the Modern Interior: From the Victorians to Today* (Oxford, New York: Berg, 2009).

8 Eugeni d'Ors [Xènius, pseud.], "La felicitat," 26 November, 1909, in Ors, *Glosari 1908-1909*, ed. Xavier Pla (Barcelona: Quaderns Crema, 2001), 668-69.

9 Letter from Rafael Masó to Esperança Bru, 9 September, 1911. Manuscript, Masó Bru family collection, Girona.

10 See Tarrús and Comadira, 146.

11 This type of simple furnishing of popular inspiration was often used by different *noucentista* architects, such as Josep Goday, who introduced it in many public schools he built and decorated. See Eva Pascual, "El mobiliari i la decoració interior de les escoles," in *Josep Goday Casals: Arquitectura escolar a Barcelona de la Mancomunitat a la República*, ed. Albert Cubeles and Marc Cuixart (Barcelona: City Council, 2008), 337-47.

12 These items of furniture are currently distributed among some children and grandchildren of the architect. The furniture designed by Rafael Masó has still not been given an exhaustive cataloguing or academic study; although some of the furniture he designed for the Masó House has often been selected as the most representative of *Noucentisme*. See Josep Mainar, *El moble català* (Barcelona: Destino, 1976), 376-92; Francesc Fontbona and Francesc Miralles, *Del Modernisme al Noucentisme*, 1888-1917, vol. 7 of the Història de l'Art Català (Barcelona: Edicions 62, 1985), 254; and the catalogue for the exhibition *Moble català* (Barcelona and Madrid: Generalitat / Electa, 1994), 332-35.

13 See Letters from Rafael Masó to Esperança Bru, 15 and 23 August, 1910; 9 December, 1910; 9, 15 and 17 May, 1911, 1 August, 1911, 23 September, 1911, 4 and 8 November, 1911. Manuscripts, Masó Bru family collection, Girona, partially published in Bernat Catllar *et al.*, *Masó explica Masó* (Girona: Col·legi d'Arquitectes de Catalunya – Demarcació de Girona, n.d.), 58-61.

14 Letter from Rafael Masó to Esperança Bru, 22 December, 1910. Manuscript, Masó Bru family collection, Girona.

15 Ibid. Underlined in the original. Partially published by Tarrús and Comadira, 60.

16 See Joaquim Folch i Torres, "Crònica: L'Exposició dels artistes Catalans a París," *La Veu de Catalunya*, 7 September, 1911, Pàgina artística; Folch, "Restauració y troballes pictòriques a Girona," *La Veu de Catalunya*, 2 February, 1911, Pàgina artística; "La restauració de Sant Salvador de Bianya," *La Veu de Catalunya*, 3, 17 and 25 August, 1911, Pàgina artística; and "El nou altar de Sant Salvador de Bianya," *La Veu de Catalunya*, 14 September, 1911, Pàgina artística.

17 See Folch, "Una exposició internacional de les arts decorative," *La Veu de Catalunya*, 19 October, 1911, Pàgina artística; and "L'interior ideal," *La Veu de Catalunya*, 8 November, 1913, Pàgina artística.

Casa Masó:
a tour

Jordi Falgàs

The narrowness of Ballesteries Street does not allow us to see the facade of the Masó House until standing before it, but once there we can see that the building is the result of joining four houses that the Masó family acquired between the mid-19th and early 20th centuries.

29

The Facade

In the periods of 1911-1912 and 1918-1919 Rafael Masó undertook two major reforms on the property until giving it its current appearance. From the first intervention, the most notable elements are the large imposing entrance and the gallery of the third floor, dating from 1912, the year he married Esperança Bru.

In the 1918 reform Masó strengthened the building's appearance of old family house, treating the facade of the ground floor with rough blocks of stone and opening three large windows with round arches, one of which would become a door after his death. Also of note is the first-floor balcony, which has been an authentic viewpoint of the life and festivals of the city during a century. On the ground floor of the house, his father and later his brother Joan ran the Impremta Masó, a printing house from which the *Diario de Gerona de avisos y noticias* was published between 1889 and 1936, and continued functioning as a printers until 1992.

Glazed ceramics is one of the most abundant and varied decorative elements in the buildings of Masó, and the house of his birth is no exception. He designed the pieces that were made by the Coromina brothers in La Gabarra factory in La Bisbal d'Empordà.

UNDACIÓ RAFAEL MASÓ

19
12

The entrance

In the reform of 1911 Masó transformed the main entrance of the house, introducing various elements alluding to history (heraldic iconography of the railing), religion (relief of Saint Narcissus and a ceramic panel of Saint Paula) and to vernacular architecture (round arches, wrought iron, glazed ceramics and stone), with the aim of consolidating the status and prestige of his family in the new bourgeois society of the period. However, Masó knew how to do it in such a way as to not produce a distorted image of the past, but his combination of materials and forms —above all the contrast of colours and textures— had a modern aspect. For example, on the small ceramic tiles of the railing he repeated up to twelve heraldic motifs that he designed from the surnames and professions of his grandparents, parents and siblings, as well as those dedicated to the street, city and the date of the work.

MASÓ

The vestibule

On the door of the first floor there is a plaque with the family surname in capital letters and a Latin cross inside a circle, two pieces designed by Masó. On entering the vestibule, the prevalence of wood and cream and chocolate colours transmits a sensation of warmth to welcome one into the house. With the repetition of vertical lengthened geometric forms (vertical strips along the plaster moulding, wainscot, and the staircase) and the light that falls from the skylight, in the background, Masó also achieved creating a sensation of large, ordered and sober space, totally in accordance with the aesthetics of the *noucentista* home. Of note is the French-made clock, from the mid-19th century, as well as the four watercolours by Guillem Roca, from the end of the same century. For the console of the living room door, on the right, Masó commissioned the sculptor Fidel Aguilar to produce a relief in wood of a typically sinuous figure with a classical air.

Prats

In the vestibule are two works by Fidel Aguilar (1894-1917), a young *noucentista* sculptor from Girona who often worked with Masó. On the left, *Goddess*, a copy reproduced by the potter Marcó in Quart c. 1920 from an original mould c. 1916. Black terracotta with *argerata* patina, 36 x 22 x 14.5 cm. Fundació Rafael Masó, reg. no. 0313. On the right, *Female Figure*, c. 1918. Painted wooden carving incorporated into the transom of the living room door, 37 x 28 x 4 cm.

The dining room

The dining room is the setting where Masó could best express the *noucentista* conception of the home: comfortable but austere, with attention to the small details but forming a harmonious whole, and full of cultured references under a humble and popular appearance. It is of no surprise, then, that some *noucentista* writers invited by the architect admired how this interior expressed the moral and aesthetic values of the Masó family. One of the basic elements of the decoration are the very thin strips of wicker that cover the walls to a height of almost two metres, crowned by a wooden shelf that goes around the whole room, and used to display small sculptures and decorative objects. Other ornamental elements that Masó introduced were the two corbels and coffered ceiling that imitates the veins of the wood. The most outstanding elements, however, are the objects designed by the architect himself, above all the imposing lamp, the coloured windows of the doors, the cupboard and the sideboard.

In the dining room is a notable collection of albarelli, old apothecary ceramic jars, possibly from the old Masó-Puig Pharmacy that Joan Masó ran. Those with a diagonal inscription could be dated to the 16th century and the others to the late 17th or the 18th centuries.

Above the sideboard the work of the *noucentista* sculptor Enric Casanovas (1882-1948) stands out, *Woman with Bundle*, c. 1906. High temperature porcelain made in the workshop of the ceramist Antoni Serra Fiter, 38.5 x 19.5 x 18 cm. Fundació Rafael Masó, reg. no. 0315.

Patrons de broderies à exécuter avec les articles de coton, lin et soie, marq
DOLLFUS-MIEG & Cie, Société anonyme
MULHOUSE-BELFORT-PARIS

The gallery and the sewing room

The galleries in the house are privileged viewpoints over the river, bridges and houses, since the Onyar traces a curve and the point of view provides a unique perspective. For the gallery, Masó designed two flower boxes of wood and metal decorated with a border and a grid, of a simple but very modern geometry. These were the spaces for sewing, stitching, darning and embroidering the huge amount of clothing in the house and of all the members of a large family such as the Masós. The architect himself often designed initials and floral or geometric decorations for pillowcases, cushions, scarves, tablecloths, bedcovers and eiderdowns that his sisters or wife sewed. Today in the sewing room there is a sample of this work, which features a tablecloth embroidered with the inscription *Tant de taula com de llit sian sempre comedit* (Always moderate for both table and bed) (1905) and the eiderdown *Fortitudo Pulchritudo* (1909).

View from the gallery of the house, looking towards the bridges that cross the Onyar. The perspective from this point places the viewer in a privileged spot, given that the river marks out a bend facing the house.

The central part of the embroidered eiderdown *Fortitudo Pulchritudo*, that Masó designed for his parents' bed, 1909. 94 x 124.5 cm. Fundació Rafael Masó, reg. no. 0030.

>
Tablecloth "*Always Moderate for Both Table and Bed*," 1905. Possibly embroidered by Angelina and Paula Masó. Cotton piqué with border finished in garland of scallop and applied crochet work. Manually sewn Yugoslavia needlework and braid stitching, in cotton threads, 61 x 66 cm, lace selvedge of 3.5 cm. Fundació Rafael Masó, reg. no. 0031.

The kitchen

The spiral staircase and kitchen tell us of the other people who also lived in the house, the cook and the maids, at the service of the Masó family. The spiral staircase is by which the maids went up and down from their rooms without having to use the main staircase; and the range cooker and plate rack recall a period in which home appliances had not yet appeared. Neither the day-to-day life nor the numerous celebrations and traditional festivals that marked the calendar could have taken place without these women, who were always occupied with the household tasks, the children, and with preparing and serving all the meals.

TENER LA CAJA BIEN CERRADA
CALDO
MAGGI
EN CUBITOS
MARCA «CRUZ-ESTRELLA»
CONTENIDO

MASÓ Y PAGÉS

GERONA

DE PRIMERA INSTANCIA É INSTRUCCIÓN

DE GERONA

Jurisdicción contenciosa

JUICIO

declarativo de menor cuantía

BOLETÍN DE LA «UNIÓN DE IMPRESORES»

Administración: Manzana, 4, principal.—Madrid.

The library and the office

Santiago Masó (1878-1960), the eldest brother of the Masó Valentí family, was who inherited the family house on the death of his parents. He gained a doctorate in law in 1903 and had an outstanding professional career as a lawyer and politician.
In 1918, his brother Rafael designed part of the furnishing for his lawyer's office, of which the large bookcase stands out. Later on, in the waiting room, which operated as the office of the articled clerk, he had shelving installed designed by Bartomeu Llongueras, an architect from Terrassa. The book and newspaper library of the Masó House is a rich and diverse example of the literary, political and professional interests of the family, and is currently available to researchers.

Prudenci Bertrana (1867-1941), *Portrait of Rafael Masó, Winner of the Natural Flower of the Girona Floral Games*, 1905. Charcoal on paper, 71.5 x 52.5 cm. Fundació Rafael Masó, reg. no. 1157.

ORÍGENES DE LA NOVELA

The living room

This living room shows a good example of the Masó House painting collection. Its origin comes from, above all, the architect's father's love for Catalan painting of the period, since, as well as being a solicitor, politician and journalist, he was also an amateur painter. Catalan landscape painting from the late-19th and early 20th centuries therefore dominates, and there are outstanding works by Laureà Barrau, Modest Urgell, Joan Brull, Antonio Graner, Baldomer Gili Roig and Iu Pascual. The furnishing in this room features the Isabelline chest of drawers and an armchair profusely decorated with embroidery that may have been brought from Cuba by Gaudenci Masó.

Modest Urgell (1839-1919), *Beach with Boats*, c. 1890. Oil on canvas, 16 x 47 cm. Fundació Rafael Masó, reg. no. 0129.

>
Iu Pascual (1883-1949), *Moonlit Night in La Garrotxa*, c. 1920 (detail). Oil on canvas, 58 x 67 cm. Fundació Rafael Masó, reg. no. 0135.

<
Laureà Barrau (1864-1957), *Highwayman*, 1880 (detall). Oil on canvas, 62 x 39 cm. Fundació Rafael Masó, reg. no. 0127.

>
Joan Brull (1863-1912), *Portrait of a Young Woman*, c. 1890. Oil on canvas, 40 x 32 cm. Fundació Rafael Masó, reg. no. 0137.

The bedrooms

The bedroom furniture on the first floor was designed by Rafael Masó in 1924, to celebrate his brother Joan's marriage. The geometric forms of the bedstead, the dressing table and the wardrobe show Masó's preference for an austere refinement and craftsman's work. For a large family such as the Masó Valentís, of course, there had been many more bedrooms in the spaces now occupied by the offices and exhibition rooms of the Foundació Rafael Masó, on the second floor. The bedroom on the second floor is dominated by a massive wardrobe-mirror and embroidery by Paula Valentí with the Holy Family.

Adolf Fargnoli (1890-1951) and Jaume Busquets (1904-1968), *Crucifix*, 1924. Wood, metal, ceramic and paint, 36 x 21.4 x 3 cm. Fundació Rafael Masó, reg. no. 0318. Busquets' Christ was included a posteriori to replace the ceramic original by Fargnoli.

The interior staircase

The interior staircase, with its pronounced verticality and geometry, is an example of how Masó adapted the English Arts & Crafts interiors to his architecture. The staircase is presided over by a ceramic panel with the image of the Virgin of the Carme, the saint of Carme Vinyals, Santiago Masó's wife.

The distribution hall of the second floor

This space houses a sample of the collection of works on paper from the Fundació Rafael Masó, with drawings by 19th-century Spanish painters that were acquired by the architect's father; some notes and sketches by Rafael Masó Pagès himself; and a project for a publicity poster, a work from Rafael Masó Valentí's youth. The massive inbuilt wardrobe is also a design by Masó, as well as the stained-glass windows of different doors, and the glazed ceramic tiles of the dado and the baseboard. From here the different bedrooms were reached, which are today occupied by the offices, the reading room, the storage rooms, and the foundation's temporary exhibition rooms.

<
Attributed to Francisco de Goya (1746-1828), *Scene from the Inquisition*, c. 1800. Watercolor on paper, 15.9 x 13.9 cm. Fundació Rafael Masó, reg. no. 0752.

>
Marià Salvador Maella (1739-1819), *Male Head*, c. 1781. Charcoal and chalk on paper, 36.2 x 29.4 cm. Fundació Rafael Masó, reg. no. 0755.

<
Vicente López (1772-1850), *Flagellation*, c. 1794. Sanguine on paper, 55 x 39 cm. Fundació Rafael Masó, reg. no. 0753.

>
Eugenio Lucas Velázquez (1817-1870), *Figures in a Landscape*, c. 1855. Watercolor and gouache on paper, 15.8 x 11 cm. Fundació Rafael Masó, reg. no. 0751.

The bathroom

Rafael Masó designed the bathroom in 1918, when his brother Santiago bought the fourth property that came to form part of the house. This box of colour is a magnificent example of how Masó combined his designs with the qualities of the materials to give character to the interiors of the home. In this case, the texture and colours of the ceramic and the mosaic, together with the stained glass of the door and window, provide a tone of warmth, hygiene and refinement to a private space that until then was not considered in the decoration of middle class homes. As well as the stained glass and glazed ceramic, the floor tiles are also the architect's design, which he had previously used in the reform of the Cendra House in Anglès.

The facade over the river

Between 1911 and 1918, while Masó was remodelling the interiors of the houses that his family had acquired, he also unified the back part to create a large facade, the widest in existence over the River Onyar. As well as painting it white to enhance the whole, he distinguished it with what he called "a graceful decor" —a large flower box in the gallery on the first floor, two ceramic panels and different horizontal strips of yellow and green glazed ceramic tiles from La Bisbal d'Empordà — wisely worked with the colours and geometry of the blinds and windows. In the final intervention he planned the characteristic crowning and the pergola of the fourth floor, two references to the vernacular architecture that he had assimilated into his work.

Rear facade of the Masó House, in an autochrome by Joan Masó from 1923.
Centre de Recerca i Difusió de la Imatge, Arxiu Històric Municipal, Ajuntament de Girona, reg. no. 25949.

The authors

Narcís-Jordi Aragó Masó, nephew of the architect Rafael Masó, has a degree in Law and a diploma in Journalism. He headed the weekly *Presència* (1967-1979) and the *Revista de Girona* (1985-2009). He has been Vice-dean of the Col·legi de Periodistes de Catalunya, and President of the Friends of the Museu d'Art de Girona. He is the author of some twenty books on subjects regarding Girona. Academic correspondent of the Reial de Belles Arts de Sant Jordi, he is the President of Honour of the Fundació Rafael Masó.

The facade of Masó House facing the River Onyar, photographer unknown, taken between the reform of 1911 and that of 1918. Fundació Rafael Masó, reg.no. 1158.

Jordi Falgàs has a PhD in Art History, and since 2008 has been the Director of the Fundació Rafael Masó. He was Assistant Executive Manager of the Fundació Gala-Salvador Dalí (1996-2003) and Cleveland Fellow at the Cleveland Museum of Art (2004-2007). He is the author of books and articles about modern and contemporary art in Catalonia, and has worked on numerous exhibitions. In 2006 he was co-curator of the exhibition *Barcelona & Modernity: Picasso, Gaudí, Miró, Dalí*, which was shown in Cleveland and at the Metropolitan Museum of Art in New York.

Rosa M. Gil Tort has a degree in Geography and History, and a Master's in Archival Studies. Between 1993 and 2011 she headed the Historic Archive of the Girona Section of the Col·legi d'Arquitectes de Catalunya. She is a member of the Editorial Board of the *Revista de Girona*, and has written diverse monographs and articles about architecture and its social context. Along the same lines she has also curated several exhibitions and, since July 2011, has been the Head of Documentation and Programs at the Fundació Rafael Masó.

Jordi Puig, photographer and publisher, is author of more than forty books on art, architecture and landscape, such as *Dalí: the Empordà Triangle*, *Barcelona Alta Costura*, *Jocs i Joguets*, *La Garrotxa* and *The Costa Brava Way*. He has also shown his work and has collaborated with some of the main museums and cultural centers in Catalonia, such as Arts Santa Mònica, the Fundació Gala-Salvador Dalí, the MUHBA, the Museu del Joguet de Catalunya, the Museu de Montserrat, the CCCB, and the Fundació "la Caixa", among others.

>
On the following page, self-portrait of Rafael Masó leaning on a chest of drawers, c. 1907. Historic Archive of the Col·legi d'Arquitectes de Catalunya – Demarcació de Girona, reg.no. 23613.